THE GRACECARD

STUDYGUIDE FOR INDIVIDUALS OR SMALL GROUPS

DISCOVER THE POWER
OF GIVING
AND RECEIVING GRACE

THE GRACE CARD

STUDY GUIDE FOR INDIVIDUALS OR SMALL GROUPS

OUTRE*CH®

TABLE OF CONTENTS

INTRODUCTION

Grace—it is the very heart of the Christian faith and the heart of our relationship with God. Grace can be defined as "God giving us what we need, not what we deserve." It is the means by which God brings Himself to us, restores us, and causes His love and His Holy Spirit to dwell within us. Every day, we also have the opportunity to rebuild relationships and heal deep wounds by extending and receiving God's grace. Through this four-week study, we hope that you will come to deeply appreciate the depth of God's grace and to witness its power in your own life and in the lives of the people around you.

THE GRACE CARD

Each one should use whatever gift he has received to serve others, faithfully administering God's grace in its various forms.

— 1 Peter 4:10

INTRODUCTION

We're glad you've chosen *The Grace Card* four-week video curriculum for you and your small group or family. *The Grace Card* study features movie clips and biblical teaching to help you better understand and extend forgiveness and grace.

The Grace Card DVD-based Study will help you:

- Extend to others the same forgiveness and grace you receive from God as a believer.

- Reflect God's love in your relationships with your family, friends, and co-workers.

- Learn to grow and mature through the lessons and teachers God sends you.

- "Get into the game" by sharing your faith and making disciples.

ABOUT *THE GRACE CARD* MOVIE

When Mac McDonald loses his son in an accident, the ensuing 17 years of bitterness and pain erode his love for his family and leave him angry with God ... and just about everyone else. Mac's rage stonewalls his career in the police department and makes for a combustible situation when he's partnered with Sam Wright, a rising star on the force who happens to be a part-time pastor and a loving family man. On top of all this, Mac's home life is as frightening as anything he encounters on the streets of Memphis. Money is tight and emotions run high as he constantly argues with his wife and his surviving son Blake, who is hanging with the wrong crowd and in danger of flunking out of school.

Sam Wright also never expected to be a police officer. He has a calling to be a minister like his Grandpa George. But leading a small, start-up church doesn't always put enough food on the table for a young family, so Sam took up another job on the police force. With his new promotion to sergeant, Sam starts questioning if his real calling might actually be police work rather than the pastorate.

Can Mac and Sam somehow join forces to help one another when they can't see past their differences—especially the most obvious one?

HOW TO USE *THE GRACE CARD* STUDY GUIDE

Use *The Grace Card* Study Guide in conjunction with *The Grace Card* DVD-based Study. If you're doing the study in an adult small group, one person in the group will need to purchase the DVD-based Study kit, which includes a Leader's Guide and a DVD with movie clips and video extras. You can also do the study on your own, with your spouse or friends, or with other members of your family. You will need to purchase *The Grace Card* DVD-based Study kit and a Study Guide for each person participating in the study.

The best way to begin *The Grace Card* study is to first watch the movie—either in a theater, at a movie event hosted by your church, or by purchasing *The Grace Card* DVD. Although *The Grace Card* DVD-based Study includes clips from the movie, watching the film in its entirety is the best way to experience the story and its message of forgiveness.

After you watch the movie, get together with your small group, family, or friends and go through each of the weekly studies. Choose a day to meet together to watch the movie clip(s) for the week and go through the discussion questions. If you're already in a small group or Sunday school class, use that time for your weekly study.

After completing each week's group study materials, complete the *On My Own* section individually, whenever it's convenient for you. Finish the *On My Own* section before you meet with your group or family for the next week's study.

FORMAT FOR *THE GRACE CARD* WEEKLY STUDIES

Each *Grace Card* weekly study is organized into sections, described below.

Prayer

We recommend that you open and close each lesson with prayer.

The Grace Card Question for the Week

Each week, your group will answer a thought-provoking question that will help everyone begin thinking about and discussing the topic for the week.

Watch

The Grace Card DVD-based Study kit includes a DVD with movie clips from the film, *The Grace Card*. There are one or more movie clips for each of the four weekly sessions.

Study and Discuss

This discussion section should make up the main portion of your meeting each week. The first part of the discussion is based on *The Grace Card* movie clip(s); the second part includes Bible passages and application questions.

Messages From *The Grace Card*

This section applies a message (theme or teaching) from the movie *The Grace Card* to your study topic for the week.

Step Into the Passage

Read these commentary-type sections for background information on the historical and cultural setting for one of the week's key Bible passages.

The Grace Card Lesson

This is a short lesson on the topic for the week, like what you might hear if you were listening to a pastor teaching on the topic of grace. You may read the lesson to yourself or, if you're doing the study as a group, ask one or more of the group members to read the lesson out loud.

On My Own

This section provides an opportunity for you to study Bible passages individually and directly apply them to your own life. After completing the week's group study, you'll want to complete the *On My Own* section before the next group meeting.

SMALL GROUP GUIDELINES

(If you are doing The Grace Card *study in a small group or Sunday school class)*

Small groups and Sunday school classes can have an enormous impact on your life and faith. They help you build friendships and provide support for your spiritual growth, and they offer you a close group of people who can encourage you and hold you accountable for strengthening your family. The guidelines below will help you get the most from your time together.

- **Confidentiality:** Remember that everything shared in your group should be considered confidential unless you are given specific permission to share it elsewhere. Confidentiality protects your group and allows it to be a supportive, accepting place for everyone.

- **Openness:** Do your best to be open and honest during discussions. Your transparency will encourage others to be the same.

- **Respect:** Everyone has the right to their opinion. All questions should be encouraged and answered in a courteous manner. Listen attentively to others without interrupting and be slow to judge. Be careful with sentences that start with "You should…" or "You ought…" and do not give advice that isn't solicited.

- **Priority:** Make the small group meeting a priority in your schedule. If you're unable to attend or are running late, call your group leader.

- **Preparedness:** Prepare your lesson and come ready to share. What you put into the lesson is what you'll get out of it!

- **Participation:** Participate in the discussion, but keep your answers brief enough to allow others to share, as well. The principle of participation says, "If there are ten people in the group, share slightly less than one-tenth of the time. If there are eight, share slightly less than one-eighth, etc."

- **Honesty:** When appropriate, offer suggestions to the leader to improve the study.

- **Connect:** Seek to know and care for other group members, as well as share transparently regarding your own emotional, spiritual, and physical needs.

- **Care:** If a member misses a session, be sure someone in the group calls to see how they're doing and to catch them up on what was missed.

- **Support:** Actively support the mission and values of the small group study and follow the directions given by your leader. Refrain from gossip and criticism; if you have concerns or questions about a member's views or statements, communicate directly and respectfully with that person.

WEEK 1:
GRACE **AWAKENING**

THIS WEEK'S QUOTE FROM THE GRACE CARD:

"Mr. Eskue taught your great-great-grandfather Wendle to read, gave him this Bible. The boy decided to be a preacher right then and there. And how many hearts were changed, how many lives? That one act of grace changed history, Sam. That is the point."

— Grandpa George talking to Sam

THIS WEEK'S SCRIPTURE:

For it is by grace you have been saved, through faith—and this not from yourselves, it is the gift of God—not by works, so that no one can boast.

— Ephesians 2:8–9

WEEK 1:
GRACE AWAKENING

Open your study with prayer.

THE GRACE CARD
QUESTION FOR THE WEEK

What is the greatest act of forgiveness you've witnessed in your lifetime? (You can choose something that happened to you personally, something you saw happen in someone else's life, or something you heard about in the news.) Share the details with your group. Also, tell your group how you reacted to that act of forgiveness. What did you think and how did you feel?

_____

_____

_____

WATCH

Watch the Week 1 movie clip on the DVD in *The Grace Card* DVD-based Study.

Grandpa George's Library *(3 minutes)*

After a discouraging Sunday service in his role as a pastor and a difficult week on the job as a police officer, Sam seeks the counsel and comfort of his grandfather George, a retired minister who was active during the days of the Civil Rights Movement. After a long walk, Grandpa George invites his grandson to his study and offers him a modern-day parable, hoping it will create the hunger in Sam to dig deeper and discover the true pearl of wisdom that has just been shared—the awesome power of God's grace.

Grandpa George's Library

STUDY
AND DISCUSS

Question 1: In this scene, Grandpa George tells Sam a story about a cotton farmer named John Eskue. Before the end of the Civil War, Mr. Eskue made a decision to free all of his slaves. Even after he freed them, most of the former slaves stayed with him. Why? How does Grandpa George explain the actions of the former slaves?

Out of love + security

Question 2: Grandpa George claims that grace changes the world, and he gives some examples in his story. Discuss some of those examples in your group. What impact did Mr. Eskue's action have on the life of Sam's great-great-grandfather, Wendle P. Wright? How did the change in Wendle's life affect Grandpa George and Sam? What about the other former slaves' and John Eskue's request that they forgive the slave owners—what impact did that have?

We hear Grandpa George tell the story about Mr. Eskue asking for forgiveness and offering grace to people who had been enslaved by him and others. He wanted to treat these children of God with honor, respect, and love. It was this grace that prompted Sam's great-great-grandfather to offer Mr. Eskue his handwritten Grace Card in return. Think of the lives changed by those "simple" acts of uncommon grace.

 Read: Ephesians 2:8–9, Romans 6:23, John 3:17, and Psalm 145:8

For it is by grace you have been saved, through faith—and this not from yourselves, it is the gift of God—not by works, so that no one can boast. —Ephesians 2:8–9

For the wages of sin is death, but the gift of God is eternal life in Christ Jesus our Lord. —Romans 6:23

For God did not send his Son into the world to condemn the world, but to save the world through him. —John 3:17

The LORD is gracious and compassionate, slow to anger and rich in love. —Psalm 145:8

Question 3: What does the gift of grace offered by George's grandfather and Mr. Eskue say about the value they placed on others? What does Christ's willingness to offer you the free gift of grace say about your value in His eyes?

Question 4: Share with your group how God's love and forgiveness has transformed your life from the time when

you first believed and accepted the gift of His grace. If you have not yet made that decision, share what it is about God's love and forgiveness that draws you to Him.

_____

_____

_____

_____

Read: Romans 3:9–12, Romans 3:21–24, Deuteronomy 32:3–4 and Romans 5:10

"There is no one righteous, not even one…" —Romans 3:10

…For all have sinned and fall short of the glory of God, and are justified freely by his grace through the redemption that came by Christ Jesus. —Romans 3:23–24

For if, when we were God's enemies, we were reconciled to him through the death of his Son, how much more, having been reconciled, shall we be saved through his life! —Romans 5:10

I will proclaim the name of the LORD. Oh, praise the greatness of our God! He is the Rock, his works are perfect, and all his ways are just. A faithful God who does no wrong, upright and just is he. —Deuteronomy 32:3–4

Question 5 : When you look at the people around you, how do you decide who is "righteous" and who isn't? How does your view contrast with God and His view of righteousness? Without Jesus, would God consider you righteous?

_____

_____

_____

Question 6 : According to the passages you've just read, have you "earned" God's grace and a place in Heaven? In Romans 5:10, the Apostle Paul reminds us that we were "enemies" of God, but we were reconciled to Him through the sacrifice of His Son. In your group, talk about how greatly you have been forgiven and what this means in your life.

_____

_____

STEP INTO THE
PASSAGE

The book of Romans is a letter the Apostle Paul wrote to Christians in Rome in approximately 57 A.D. At that time, there was a large Jewish population in the city of Rome, and the Christian Church was a mix of Jewish and Gentile (non-Jewish) believers.

In Romans 3, Paul made it clear that all have sinned—Gentiles and Jews alike—and that God extends His grace and forgiveness to all. This was a difficult concept for the Jewish Christians, for they viewed themselves as chosen by God—and in fact, they were. God had chosen the Jewish people as a holy nation. Deuteronomy 14:2 reads, "...For you are a people holy to the LORD your God. Out of all the peoples on the face of the earth, the LORD has chosen you to be his treasured possession." But the Jews had also been instructed that the Messiah (Jesus) would provide salvation for the Gentiles. "I will also make you a light for the Gentiles, that you may bring my salvation to the ends of the earth" (Isaiah 49:6).

In Acts 10, 11, and 15, you can read about the assimilation of the Gentiles into the Christian Church. In Acts 10, the Apostle Peter was called to Caesarea to meet an Italian centurion named Cornelius, and Peter witnessed God pouring out His Holy Spirit on the Gentiles. In Acts 15, the leaders of the Christian Church—Peter, Jesus' brother James, and Paul—all affirmed that God had fulfilled His promise and brought salvation to the Gentiles.

Through Jesus, we (Gentiles) have been adopted into God's family!

Caesarea Palace

Question 7: Read the Step Into the Passage section for some cultural and historical background on Romans 3. The Jewish people had been chosen by God, and yet through Jesus the Gentiles were also offered grace and salvation. It took some convincing for the first (Jewish) Christians to believe that Gentiles could be a part of God's kingdom. In Romans 3, what does the Bible say about how God extends His grace not only to you, but to people who are different from you? Are there people you view in the same way the Jews viewed the Gentiles—as somehow ineligible for God's grace? What can you do to change the way you see them?

_____

_____

_____

THE GRACE CARD
LESSON

For it is by grace you have been saved, through faith—and this not from yourselves, it is the gift of God—not by works, so that no one can boast. —Ephesians 2:8–9

Read the following lesson to yourself, or if you're doing the study as a group, ask one or more of the group members to read the lesson out loud.

To understand the Christian life, you must understand grace. It is the heart of our faith and the heart of our relationship with God. Grace is the means by which God brings Himself to us and restores us. Grace is best defined as "God giving us what we need, not what we deserve." We deserve to be punished for our sins, but in grace, God offers us forgiveness. Through forgiveness, we are able to experience blessing upon blessing. Grace is a gift that is totally undeserved, but which we can accept in faith. We tend to offer people conditional love: "I love you if..." But Jesus Christ offers each of us unconditional love: "I love you, period!" When we are the recipients of such an awesome gift, our hearts are transformed and the desire of our hearts becomes helping others understand amazing grace.

Gratitude should be one of the defining characteristics of those who are the recipients of such lavish grace. We are instructed in God's Word, in our gratitude for what Christ has done for us, to treat others with the same respect and honor with which we ourselves would want to be treated. Remember the Golden Rule: Do unto others as you would have them do unto you. Grandpa George is trying to teach Sam that forgiveness and grace are to be offered even to those who seem undeserving. Grace is a powerful offense against the evil attacks of this world: Each one should use whatever gift he has received to serve others, faithfully administering God's grace in its various forms (1 Peter 4:10).

When we sin, hurt those around us, or turn away from God's commands, He is always full of grace and willing to receive us back in love and mercy. We all need God. "The most important thing is that I complete my mission, the work that the Lord Jesus gave me—to tell people the Good News about God's grace," says Paul in Acts 20:24b (NCV). Sharing the transforming grace of God with others is a sacred responsibility. It has the power to transform lives! To whom is God calling you to extend love and grace?

STUDY
AND **DISCUSS**

Read: 1 Corinthians 15:9–10 and John 15:5–12

For I am the least of the apostles and do not even deserve to be called an apostle, because I persecuted the church of God. But by the grace of God I am what I am, and his grace to me was not without effect. No, I worked harder than all of them— yet not I, but the grace of God that was with me. —1 Corinthians 15:9–10

My command is this: Love each other as I have loved you. —John 15:12

Question 8: The passage in 1 Corinthians 15 was written by the Apostle Paul, who before his conversion to Christianity persecuted the Church and had many Christians arrested and killed. Yet, Jesus through His grace chose Paul to follow Him and spread the good news of the Gospel. What impact did God's forgiveness and grace have on Paul? How did the Apostle Paul change the lives of others?

_____

_____

Question 9: Earlier, we talked about how greatly we are loved and valued by God. How would it change the way you look at people if you saw them the same way God does? Are certain people easier (and others harder) for you to view as valuable and worth loving? Why do you think that is?

_____

_____

_____

Question 10: In the John 15 passage, Jesus commands us to love one another. What additional instruction does He give about how we can love others? What are some ways in which you can "remain" (some translations say "abide") in Jesus and let His joy and love flow through you?

Ask group members to share prayer requests, and then close your study with prayer.

REMEMBER TO COMPLETE THE **ON MY OWN** SECTION BEFORE YOUR NEXT GROUP MEETING.

ON MY OWN

A key component of grace is forgiveness, and you can witness the need for forgiveness throughout *The Grace Card*. Mac has held onto his anger over the death of his son, and his bitterness continually spills over into his relationships with his fellow police officers, with anyone who is African American, and even with his own wife and son. The lack of forgiveness has almost destroyed Mac's family, as his son Blake rebels and his wife blames him for the strained relationships. Even Sam struggles with seeing Mac through God's eyes and forgiving Mac for the times that he "can feel white eyes burning through his black skin just because of that black skin."

Sam challenges his congregation by preaching about loving others, and then asks, "What if it's somebody who just plain don't like you?" God has forgiven us and poured out His grace and His love for us. How easy is it—really—to love others and forgive them when they hurt us? How can we offer grace to those who don't deserve our forgiveness?

Question 1: Which person in your life has been the hardest to forgive? Which person has been the easiest to forgive? What made it easy to forgive the one person and hard to forgive the other?

Question 2: What's your definition of forgiveness? In your life, how have you "forgiven" people?

 Read: Hebrews 10:30–31 and re-read Romans 6:23

For we know him who said, "It is mine to avenge; I will repay," and again, "The Lord will judge his people." It is a dreadful thing to fall into the hands of the living God. —Hebrews 10:30–31

For the wages of sin is death, but the gift of God is eternal life in Christ Jesus our Lord. —Romans 6:23

FORGIVENESS

for-give [fer-giv]: to grant pardon for or remission of (an offense, debt, etc.); absolve. (Source: Dictionary.com)

What is forgiveness? Forgiveness does not mean that a harm done to us was *not* wrong, or that when we've been hurt, it doesn't matter. Our God is a God of justice, and wrongs deserve punishment. What forgiveness *does* mean is that we voluntarily give up our right to repay a wrong, and we leave justice to God. Forgiveness is a conscious decision to let go of anger and the desire to punish the other person. In some cases, when a person has hurt us badly and that pain has had a long-lasting impact, forgiveness could be a long process. If angry feelings re-occur or if a person hurts us again, we might need to confront the feelings, give them to God, and once again extend forgiveness and grace.

Question 3: Consider the penalty for sin: In Romans 6:23, the Apostle Paul says the wages of sin is death. Now, think about the person you find hardest to forgive. Would you want that person to suffer the penalty for sin, or would you want them to receive mercy? Which one has God given you?

_____

_____

_____

 Read: Colossians 3:13, Mark 11:25-26, and Matthew 18:21-35

Bear with each other and forgive whatever grievances you may have against one another. Forgive as the Lord forgave you. —Colossians 3:13

And when you stand praying, if you hold anything against anyone, forgive him, so that your Father in heaven may forgive you your sins. —Mark 11:25-26

Then the master called the servant in. "You wicked servant," he said, "I canceled all that debt of yours because you begged me to. Shouldn't you have had mercy on your fellow servant just as I had on you?" —Matthew 18:32-33

Question 4: As you read these verses, does forgiveness sound like a suggestion or a command? If you refuse to forgive someone, how does that choice affect your relationship with God?

_____

_____

_____

 Read: Luke 23:33-34, Romans 5:10, and Philippians 2:5-8

When they came to the place called the Skull, there they crucified him, along with the criminals—one on his right, the other on his left. Jesus said, "Father, forgive them, for they do not know what they are doing." —Luke 23:33-34

For if, when we were God's enemies, we were reconciled to him through the death of his Son, how much more, having been reconciled, shall we be saved through his life! —Romans 5:10

Your attitude should be the same as that of Christ Jesus: Who, being in very nature God, did not consider equality with God something to be grasped, but made himself nothing, taking the very nature of a servant, being made in human likeness. And being found in appearance as a man, he humbled himself and became obedient to death—even death on a cross! —Philippians 2:5-8

Question 5 : The free gift of grace comes only through Christ. It is a free gift, but not a cheap gift. While we were "enemies" of God, Jesus humbled Himself to the point of becoming human, dwelled on earth, and suffered a painful, humiliating death. Yet, Christ forgave even while He was on the cross. Take a few moments to think about the "cost" of forgiveness. What does it cost you emotionally to forgive someone? What do you gain from it?

_____

_____

_____

Question 6 : Grandpa George's own grandfather wrote these words as a boy: "I promise to pray for you every day, ask your forgiveness, grant you the same, and be your friend always." To whom do you need to offer a "Grace Card"? Below, write the name(s) of anyone you need to forgive, the hurt for which you're forgiving them, and your next steps.

NAME	I AM FORGIVING THIS PERSON FOR...	NEXT STEP(S)

In some cases, you might not be able to contact the person, or it's not safe or healthy to do so. That's all right—you can forgive the person before God and release the anger you've felt toward them. In other cases, your next step will be to contact the person, tell them you have forgiven them, and offer them a Grace Card.

PRAYER FOR GRACE

Below is a suggested prayer for this study. You're welcome to use all of it, some of it, or compose your own prayer thanking God for His grace and telling Him about those to whom you're offering forgiveness. Whichever you choose, we recommend that you close your time of study and devotion by talking with the God who loves you beyond all understanding.

"Lord, I am so grateful for your forgiveness and your grace. I confess that I am a sinner, and you have offered me the free gift of salvation, though it cost you the weight of my sins and the pain of crucifixion. Your sacrifice has set me free and given me new life and an eternity with you. Thank you for your love and for transforming my life through the incredible power of your grace. Lord, I have heard your command that I am to forgive others as you have forgiven me. Before you now, I forgive _____ and I release him/her to you. I wish to release my anger, and I give up my claim against them. Lord, forgive me of my sins, as well, and wash any anger and bitterness from my heart. Soothe the hurt I have suffered by them, and pour your love and your grace into me. I pray that you empower me through your Holy Spirit to see others as you see them—to value them and love them as you would. Lord, bless me and guide me so that I may offer grace to those you've placed in my life. Accomplish great things through my life, Lord, I pray. Amen."

Notes

Prayer Request
(Kris)
     Zee - son angry @ God
        over loss of baby
(Ashley)
Sharon - Daughter - Crone's disease

Charlie - tempted to go back to drinking

Dale - broken hearted people

WEEK 2:
GRACE **OVERFLOWING**

THIS WEEK'S QUOTE
FROM THE GRACE CARD:

"Just once, I wanted to have a normal conversation with you instead of another stinkin' fight. Why do you think I go somewhere else every night? I don't need this!"

— Blake to Mac

THIS WEEK'S SCRIPTURE:

"You are the salt of the earth. But if the salt loses its saltiness, how can it be made salty again? It is no longer good for anything, except to be thrown out and trampled by men. You are the light of the world. A city on a hill cannot be hidden."

— Matthew 5:13-14

THE GRACECARD

WEEK 2:
GRACE **OVERFLOWING**

Open your study with prayer.

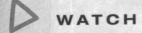

THE GRACE CARD
QUESTION FOR THE WEEK

Think of the person who has influenced you the most. What kind of example did that person provide for you, and how did they influence your personality, the course of your life, and your reactions to other people? Share your answer with your group.

_____

_____

_____

▷ WATCH

Watch the Week 2 movie clips on the DVD in *The Grace Card* DVD-based Study. There are two clips for this week.

Dinner at the McDonald House

Dinner at the Wright House

Dinner at the McDonald House *(2½ minutes)*

In what has become a rare instance at the McDonald house, Blake joins his parents for dinner in an attempt to connect with his dad. Unfortunately, Blake also needs to break the news to his father that his elite private school has asked him to leave. Mac explodes in rage, screaming at both his son and his wife. "Just once, I wanted to have a normal conversation with you instead of another stinkin' fight," Blake says before walking out of the house. Mac then storms out of the room, leaving Sara to once again pick up the pieces.

Dinner at the Wright House *(2:02 minutes)*

Sam Wright is home with his family and is working on his sermon for the weekend. He's interrupted by his daughters but is lovingly treated by his wife, who encourages him to finish his work and join the family for dinner. The Wright family prays together before the meal, and then Debra breaks the news of Sam's high cholesterol and unappealing new diet.

STUDY
AND DISCUSS

Question 1: Both of these clips show family dinners, but the atmosphere and the conversation at these two dinners is vastly different. List the differences you see between the two families. In your group, discuss the contrast you see between the McDonald and Wright families. What is the key difference?

_____

_____

_____

Question 2: Without a relationship with God and the power of His grace, Mac cannot find healing from the pain of his son's death. Instead, Mac's bitterness permeates his life and overflows into all of his relationships. How does Mac's anger impact his relationship with his wife? How does it affect his relationship with Blake?

_____

_____

_____

Question 3: Imagine that you could stop the scene right when Blake confesses to his father that he's been asked to leave his school. If Mac had calmly asked for Blake to explain what happened, and then offered his son grace and understanding, how do you think this scene might have ended?

_____

_____

_____

 Read: Luke 6:45 and Galatians 5:19–23.

"The good man brings good things out of the good stored up in his heart, and the evil man brings evil things out of the evil stored up in his heart. For out of the overflow of his heart his mouth speaks." —Luke 6:45

The acts of the sinful nature are obvious: sexual immorality, impurity and debauchery; idolatry and witchcraft; hatred, discord, jealousy, fits of rage, selfish ambition, dissensions, factions and envy; drunkenness, orgies, and the like. I warn you, as I did before, that those who live like this will not inherit the kingdom of God. But the fruit of the Spirit is love, joy, peace, patience, kindness, goodness, faithfulness, gentleness and self-control. —Galatians 5:19–23

Paul gives a good example of leaving a multiple-generation legacy in 2 Timothy 1:5: *I have been reminded of your sincere faith, which first lived in your grandmother Lois and in your mother Eunice and, I am persuaded, now lives in you also.*

Sam and Mac are creating very different legacies through their influence on their children. Mac rejects God and harbors bitterness in his heart. Sam lives for God and sets an example for his daughters through his teaching and his treatment of them and their mother.

What kind of legacy are you leaving those who are looking to you? What family member has left a godly legacy for you? Thank that person this week.

Question 4: The statement "out of the overflow of his heart his mouth speaks" (other translations read "out of the abundance of the heart") is an important principle. How can you see this principle illustrated in Mac's life? Can you think of a time in your own life when pain, anger, or bitterness in your heart overflowed into what you said to another person? How did your words affect your relationship with that person?

_____

_____

_____

Question 5: Compare the acts of the sinful nature with the fruit of the Spirit in Galatians 5. If a person does not live in obedience to God nor allow His Spirit to flow through them, how might they treat other people? In contrast, when a person lives by faith and spends time reading the Bible, praying, and listening to God, how can the Holy Spirit impact their behavior and relationships? Give a specific example.

_____

_____

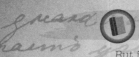 **Read: 1 John 1:5-7 and Matthew 5:13-16**

> But if we walk in the light, as he is in the light, we have
> fellowship with one another, and the blood of Jesus, his Son,
> purifies us from all sin.   —1 John 1:7

> "You are the salt of the earth. But if the salt loses its
> saltiness, how can it be made salty again? It is no longer good for
> anything, except to be thrown out and trampled by men. You are
> the light of the world. A city on a hill cannot be hidden. Neither
> do people light a lamp and put it under a bowl. Instead they put
> it on its stand, and it gives light to everyone in the house.
> In the same way, let your light shine before men, that
> they may see your good deeds and praise your
> Father in heaven."   —Matthew 5:13-16

Question 6: According to 1 John 1:7, what is the source
of true fellowship? Would you say you are "walking in the
light"? Does that light show up in your relationships? Why
or why not?

_____

_____

_____

Question 7: Use the teaching in Matthew 5 as a way to
evaluate your impact on the world around you. *(Read Step
Into the Passage for some background on how salt was
used in first century Israel.)* Remember that salt flavors and
preserves. Light chases away darkness and reveals what
is true and good. Put a ✓ next to the statement that best
reflects your life and your relationships right now. Share your
answer with your group.

___ I don't have a relationship with God yet.

___ I'm a little bit salty, but I need to be more consistent.

___ I've lost my saltiness.

___ My light shines before others and glorifies God.

Salt had a variety of uses in the first century and was vitally important for life in ancient Israel. It was used to season food and make its flavor more appealing. Salt was also used as a preservative, to keep meat and other foods fresh in a time before electricity and modern freezers. Finally, it was used as a fertilizer and weed killer. In Ezra 6:9, there is a list of basic necessities for the people working on the Temple in Jerusalem. Look at what the list includes: *Whatever is needed—young bulls, rams, male lambs for burnt offerings to the God of heaven, and wheat, salt, wine and oil, as requested by the priests in Jerusalem—must be given them daily without fail...* Clearly, salt was a critical element for life during Jesus' ministry.

When Jesus compares His disciples to salt, think about the implications. Christ-followers (Christians) are vitally important for life in this world!

Salt at the edge of the Dead Sea

THE GRACE CARD
LESSON

 Re-read: Matthew 5:13–16

"You are the salt of the earth. But if the salt loses its saltiness, how can it be made salty again? It is no longer good for anything, except to be thrown out and trampled by men. You are the light of the world. A city on a hill cannot be hidden. Neither do people light a lamp and put it under a bowl. Instead they put it on its stand, and it gives light to everyone in the house. In the same way, let your light shine before men, that they may see your good deeds and praise your Father in heaven."   —Matthew 5:13–16

Read the following lesson to yourself, or if you're doing the study as a group, ask one or more of the group members to read the lesson out loud.

In 1 John 1:7, we read: ... *if we walk in the light, as he is in the light, we have fellowship with one another...* There are a couple of key words to highlight: *if* and *fellowship*. On a positive note, *if* we are walking with Christ, then we have strong relationships with others, centered on our love for Christ.

On the other hand, *if* our relationship with Christ is non-existent or deteriorating, then this will have a negative effect on every other relationship we have. Mac is a good illustration of this principle. In the aftermath of tragedy, Mac has allowed anger and bitterness to poison his life, as well as the lives of his son and his wife. He has become a bitter person whom no one wants to be near.

Our relationship with Christ—or lack thereof—affects every other relationship we have. If we have a strong relationship with Jesus, our relationships will reflect it. If we don't, our relationships will suffer as a result.

In Matthew 5:13–14, Jesus tells his believers that: *"You are the salt of the earth. ... You are the light of the world ..."* In Mark 9:50, Jesus says: *"Salt is good, but if it loses its saltiness, how can you make it salty again? Have salt in yourselves, and be at peace with each other."*

Have you ever thought about how pervasive salt can be? A little salt can totally alter the taste of bland food. How about light? In the deepest, darkest caverns of the earth, one small flame can pierce the darkness. The Bible also uses the example of yeast in a batch of dough; a small amount of yeast will cause the entire batch of dough to rise during baking. Jesus has called His followers to be salt and light to the world; if you are a believer, *you* are a living testament to the transforming power of His grace.

Finally, remember that it is God and the presence of His Holy Spirit within a believer that enables that person to become salt and light to the people in their life—to co-workers, neighbors, spouse, and children. If the fruit of His Spirit—love, peace, patience, self-control—are at work within you, only then can you truly lift up your family and friends and show them the Savior who can transform them and give them eternal life.

STUDY AND **DISCUSS**

Read: 1 Corinthians 13:4-7

Love is patient, love is kind. It does not envy, it does not boast, it is not proud. It is not rude, it is not self-seeking, it is not easily angered, it keeps no record of wrongs. Love does not delight in evil but rejoices with the truth. It always protects, always trusts, always hopes, always perseveres. —1 Corinthians 13:4-7

Question 8 : In what ways do you show this type of love and grace to your spouse? Do you "keep a record of wrongs," or do you offer grace and forgiveness? If you're not married, how does this description compare to the way you treat the people closest to you? Which part(s) of this description (e.g., patience, anger, keeping record of wrongs) do you most need to work on?

_____

_____

_____

 Read: Psalm 78:4-7, 2 Timothy 1:5, and Proverbs 14:26

...We will tell the next generation the praiseworthy deeds of the LORD, his power, and the wonders he has done. He decreed statutes for Jacob and established the law in Israel, which he commanded our forefathers to teach their children, so the next generation would know them, even the children yet to be born, and they in turn would tell their children. Then they would put their trust in God and would not forget his deeds but would keep his commands.   —Psalm 78:4-7

I have been reminded of your sincere faith, which first lived in your grandmother Lois and in your mother Eunice and, I am persuaded, now lives in you also.   —2 Timothy 1:5

He who fears the LORD has a secure fortress, and for his children it will be a refuge.   —Proverbs 14:26

Question 9 : In what ways are Sam Wright and his wife Debra a good illustration for these passages? What are they teaching their daughters about following God and how to treat others?

_____

_____

_____

Question 10 : What are some specific ways you can demonstrate grace within your own family? In particular, if you have children, how can you raise your children to be salt and light in this world? Give a specific example from an issue you're currently facing.

_____

_____

_____

Ask group members to share prayer requests, and then close your study with prayer.

REMEMBER TO COMPLETE THE **ON MY OWN** SECTION BEFORE YOUR NEXT GROUP MEETING.

ON MY OWN

The biggest difference between the two families in the film wasn't the family prayer or the presence or absence of laughter, and it wasn't whether there was a disagreement over dinner. The biggest difference between the two families was the presence of the Holy Spirit. The Wrights followed God and taught their children to do the same. The Bible teaches us that we love others because God first loved us and because His Spirit resides within us through faith. The best-known verse in the Bible tells us how powerful God's love is: *For God so loved the world that he gave his one and only Son, that whoever believes in him shall not perish but have eternal life* (John 3:16). And without God's love in your heart, you cannot truly express love and grace to the people around you.

Question 1: As a follower of Christ, you have God's Holy Spirit within you. How has God worked through His Spirit to change you? In what ways are you different from the person you were before becoming a Christian?

_____

_____

_____

If you have not yet accepted Jesus into your life, think about the Christians you know. Is there a Christian whose life and behavior has changed through their relationship with God? What changes have you seen in them?

If you would like to become a follower of Christ and experience His love in your life, share your desire with your group leader.

 Read: 1 John 4:7–17 and Romans 5:5

This is love: not that we loved God, but that he loved us and sent his Son as an atoning sacrifice for our sins. Dear friends, since God so loved us, we also ought to love one another. No one has ever seen God; but if we love one another, God lives in us and his love is made complete in us. —1 John 4:10–12

And hope does not disappoint us, because God has poured out his love into our hearts by the Holy Spirit, whom he has given us. —Romans 5:5

Question 2: According to Romans 5:5, what is the true source of the love we feel for others?

Question 3: In what ways have you struggled to consistently love the people closest to you? Does your treatment of them change according to your feelings?

Question 4: Think about a time when you clearly felt God's love for you. Did that awareness of God's love affect your treatment of others? How?

Re-read: Matthew 5:13–16

"You are the salt of the earth. But if the salt loses its saltiness, how can it be made salty again? It is no longer good for anything, except to be thrown out and trampled by men. You are the light of the world. A city on a hill cannot be hidden. Neither do people light a lamp and put it under a bowl. Instead they put it on its stand, and it gives light to everyone in the house. In the same way, let your light shine before men, that they may see your good deeds and praise your Father in heaven." —Matthew 5:13–16

Question 5: In the table below, write the names of one or two people for each type (friend, family, co-worker/neighbor) of relationship. Then, put a ✓ in one of the middle columns to indicate whether you are "salt and light" in that relationship. In the right column, explain your answer.

NAME	ARE YOU SALT/LIGHT?		EXPLANATION
FRIENDS (LIST ONE OR TWO)	YES	NO	
FAMILY MEMBERS	YES	NO	
CO-WORKERS OR NEIGHBORS	YES	NO	

(**NOTE:** When Jesus said, "You are the salt of the earth," He was talking to His followers. If you have not made a decision to follow Christ, you can leave this question blank and come back to it when you're ready. If you are a new believer, name some people for whom you could be "salt and light" now that you know Christ.)

Question 6 : Choose one or two relationships in the list above. Commit to reflecting Jesus to that person (or people) this week. Think of some specific ways in which you can show them God's love and grace.

PRAYER FOR GRACE

"Lord, your love and your grace are amazing! When you came to earth and sacrificed yourself, you saved me and gave me eternal life—a life that is forever with you. God, I want the people around me to experience that same eternity. Please pour your love and your Spirit into me and enable me to love others through you. I want to lift up my relationship with _____ and ask you to help me see them through your eyes. Help me treat them with grace this week. Give me discernment and empower me to sense their feelings and their needs, so that I may be salt and light in their life. Lord, you have given me love and life, and I am yours. Use me and work through me to bring light to the world. I pray this in your Son's name, Amen."

Notes

WEEK 3:
GRACE LESSONS

THIS WEEK'S QUOTE FROM THE GRACE CARD:

"I don't know about you, but it sure seems to me that when God's got something to teach me, he brings me a teacher. But I don't usually like the lesson, and I usually don't like being taught."

— Sam to his congregation

THIS WEEK'S SCRIPTURE:

Consider it pure joy, my brothers, whenever you face trials of many kinds, because you know that the testing of your faith develops perseverance. Perseverance must finish its work so that you may be mature and complete, not lacking anything.

— James 1:2-4

THE GRACE CARD

WEEK 3:
GRACE **LESSONS**

Open your study with prayer.

THE GRACE CARD
QUESTION FOR THE WEEK

What do you think is the most difficult character trait (e.g., humility, patience, generosity, self-control) to obtain? Why? Give an example from your own life.

_____

_____

_____

WATCH

Watch the Week 3 movie clips on the DVD in *The Grace Card* DVD-based Study. There are two movie clips this week.

Sam's Sermon *(4:22 minutes)*
Sam has just finished a difficult first week with Mac as his new partner, and he is struggling to love a man who not only isn't lovable, but just plain doesn't like him... or his color. It's a difficult lesson to learn—that although some people don't seem to deserve love or grace, we're called to offer it anyway. God has laid it on Sam's heart to share this truth with his congregation, but it doesn't take long to realize the congregation doesn't like the lesson any more than Sam.

Sam's Sermon

Standing Room at Gospel Church (4:22 *minutes*)

Six weeks after preaching a very difficult message about unconditional love and grace, Sam has recovered from surgery and is back in the pulpit. This time, however, he's preaching to a packed house full of new faces—and those faces are of every color and race. Their senior pastor has taught the congregation of Gospel Church a lesson on grace, and Sam has taught the lesson through his actions even more than through his words. As he starts his sermon, Sam acknowledges Mac—the "professor" God sent to first teach the lesson to him.

Sam's Sermon

STUDY
AND DISCUSS

Question 1: Someone once applied a famous quote to the job of a pastor, saying that pastors "comfort the afflicted and afflict the comfortable."[1] In the first scene, Sam started his sermon by warning the congregation that his message wouldn't be "an easy one to swallow, much less to follow." In what ways did Sam disturb his congregation's "comfortable" view of love? Did Sam's words affect your own views on the nature of love?

_____

_____

_____

Question 2: Do you think pastors should preach lessons that are uncomfortable to hear and difficult to follow? Why or why not? Give an example of a message you've heard in church or somewhere else that was difficult for you to swallow and follow.

_____

_____

_____

Question 3: In the second scene, Sam's church has changed, and the congregation is open to his message on love and grace. What do you think caused the change?

_____

_____

_____

 Read: James 1:2-4 and Romans 5:3-5

Consider it pure joy, my brothers, whenever you face trials of many kinds, because you know that the testing of your faith develops perseverance. Perseverance must finish its work so that you may be mature and complete, not lacking anything. —James 1:2-4

[1] The original quote was from American writer and humorist Finley Peter Dunne, who said the newspaper, "...comforts th' afflicted, afflicts th' comfortable..."

In the first movie clip for this week, Sam speaks to his congregation about the true meaning of loving others. In the course of the film, though, Sam doesn't just talk about love and grace, he demonstrates it by reaching out to a family that needs him, and being willing to endure personal sacrifice. Jesus not only spoke of love, He went to the cross to save us and to show us that, *"God so loved the world that he gave his one and only Son..."* (John 3:16). This week, what can you do to love others?

> Not only so, but we also rejoice in our sufferings, because we know that suffering produces perseverance; perseverance, character; and character, hope. And hope does not disappoint us, because God has poured out his love into our hearts by the Holy Spirit, whom he has given us. —Romans 5:3–5

Question 4 : In his sermon, Sam confesses his attitude toward lessons from God: "I don't usually like the lesson, and I usually don't like being taught." Mac is helping Sam learn about unconditional love and grace, but spending time in Mac's company is definitely a "trial" for Sam. In your own words, summarize what James 1:2–4 says about "trials." How can they change us?

_____

_____

_____

Question 5 : Look at some of the words used in Romans 5 and James 1 describing how trials affect and develop us. Those words include *mature, complete, perseverance, character, hope.* Choose one or two of these words and describe how a trial in your life helped you develop that description or characteristic.

_____

_____

John 8:1–11 tells the story of two very different types of "teachers." You can read the full account in your Bible or the excerpted version below. In this story, the Pharisees brought an adulterous woman to Jesus, hoping to trap Him into disobeying the Jewish laws.

The teachers of the law and the Pharisees brought in a woman caught in adultery. They made her stand before the group and said to Jesus, "Teacher, this woman was caught in the act of adultery. In the Law Moses commanded us to stone such women. Now what do you say?"

He ... said to them, "If any one of you is without sin, let him be the first to throw a stone at her." ... At this, those who heard began to go away one at a time, the older ones first, until only Jesus was left, with the woman still standing there. Jesus ... asked her, "Woman, where are they? Has no one condemned you?" "No one, sir," she said. "Then neither do I condemn you," Jesus declared. "Go now and leave your life of sin."

The name Pharisee means "separated one," and the Pharisees considered themselves righteous and above the rest of the Israelite people. There were about six thousand Pharisees at the time of Jesus' ministry, and they held strictly to Mosaic laws (traditional Jewish laws given by Moses). While the Pharisees publicly obeyed the letter of the law, they did not let the true spirit of the law work its way into their hearts. They were legalistic, self-righteous, and quick to condemn the woman in this story.

Contrast their behavior to Jesus' actions. The Son of God, who truly does have the power and right to judge, instead offered grace and acceptance to the woman. Who was the real Teacher in this story?

Model of the Temple in Jerusalem— the setting for John 8

 Read: Ephesians 4:11–13 and Philippians 4:9

It was he who gave some to be apostles, some to be prophets, some to be evangelists, and some to be pastors and teachers, to prepare God's people for works of service, so that the body of Christ may be built up until we all reach unity in the faith and in the knowledge of the Son of God and become mature, attaining to the whole measure of the fullness of Christ. —Ephesians 4:11–13

Whatever you have learned or received or heard from me, or seen in me—put it into practice. And the God of peace will be with you. —Philippians 4:9

Question 6: Grandpa George and Mac are very different kinds of "teachers," but they both helped Sam learn about grace. What kind of a teacher is Grandpa George? In what ways does he illustrate the two passages you just read?

_____

_____

_____

Question 7: Is there anyone in your life who teaches God's Word through both their words and their actions? What can you do to spend more time around people who have a mature relationship with God and can help you learn and grow?

_____

_____

_____

THE GRACE CARD
LESSON

 Re-read: James 1:2-4

Consider it pure joy, my brothers, whenever you face trials of many kinds, because you know that the testing of your faith develops perseverance. Perseverance must finish its work so that you may be mature and complete, not lacking anything. —James 1:2-4

Read the following lesson to yourself, or if you're doing the study as a group, ask one or more of the group members to read the lesson out loud.

In his Sunday morning sermon, Sam offers a very difficult but profound lesson. What we know we should do—from reading God's Word and from the work of the Holy Spirit in our hearts—is not always what we do in real-life situations. In this specific example, Sam is talking about love. His congregation is quick to affirm that God calls us to love others. But when Sam begins to challenge them about how far they're willing to go to demonstrate God's love and grace, the sermon that started with appreciation and shouts of "Amen!" from his church members ends with silence and awkward handshakes outside the church.

James 1:2–4 refers to Jesus' followers becoming "mature and complete, not lacking anything." When Sam starts his sermon, are the Christians in his congregation mature when it comes to the love in their hearts? Would you say they are "complete and not lacking anything" when they are called to offer God's grace to people who do not love or accept them in return? What about Sam himself? As he partners with Mac, Sam comes to realize that even as a pastor and a leader of God's church, he isn't fully able to love people who seem unlovable—and especially those who view him with prejudice and anger.

The Bible tells us that God disciplines and teaches us in much the same way a father teaches the child in whom he delights. In *The Grace Card*, Sam learns a lesson about love from several "teachers." One teacher is Mac, who causes Sam to confront his own lack of love, and at the same time shows Sam how greatly other people need the grace and forgiveness available from Jesus Christ. God also instructs Sam through the wise counsel of Grandpa George and the loving input of Sam's wife, Debra.

As you examine your own life, is there anything God is trying to teach you? Are you open to learning from God through trials and through the influence of God's teachers? As you confront new lessons in your life, remember God's Word: *Blessed is the man you discipline, O LORD, the man you teach from your law…* (Psalm 94:12).

STUDY
AND **DISCUSS**

Read: Proverbs 3:11–12, Proverbs 9:9–10, and John 6:45

My son, do not despise the LORD's discipline and do not resent his rebuke, because the LORD disciplines those he loves, as a father the son he delights in. —Proverbs 3:11–12

Instruct a wise man and he will be wiser still; teach a righteous man and he will add to his learning. The fear of the LORD is the beginning of wisdom, and knowledge of the Holy One is understanding. —Proverbs 9:9–10

"It is written in the Prophets: 'They will all be taught by God.' Everyone who listens to the Father and learns from him comes to me." —John 6:45

Question 8: After reading these passages, how do you feel about learning from God? What part does that learning play in the life of a Christ-follower?

_____

_____

_____

Question 9: According to Proverbs 9:9–10, what is the true source of wisdom? How do you build up your own wisdom and understanding?

_____

_____

_____

Question 10: Name one or two truths or personal characteristics you think God would have you learn this year. Are there any challenges (or teachers) in your life that could help you learn these lessons? What are the challenges, and who are the teachers?

_____

_____

_____

Ask group members to share prayer requests, and then close your study with prayer.

REMEMBER TO COMPLETE THE **ON MY OWN** SECTION BEFORE YOUR NEXT GROUP MEETING.

ON MY OWN

During his sermon, Sam confesses that when God wants to teach him, "I don't usually like the lesson, and I usually don't like being taught." Resistance to trials and hard lessons is quite simply a part of our human nature. Learning to love people who dislike us, giving grace to those who don't deserve it, and forgiving people who have greatly hurt us can seem to take more conviction and love than we have. Fortunately, God doesn't ask us to grow and mature using only our own power and determination. He provides the teachers, the trials, and His Holy Spirit within us. What we need to be is … willing.

Question 1: Below, list a few of the most important life lessons you've learned in the last five years. Beside each one, write a note about what (or who) taught you that lesson.

_____

_____

_____

 Read: Proverbs 15:5 and Deuteronomy 5:16

Only a fool despises a parent's discipline;
whoever learns from correction is wise. —Proverbs 15:5 (NLT)

"Honor your father and your mother, as the LORD your God has
commanded you, so that you may live long and that it
may go well with you…" —Deuteronomy 5:16

Question 2: What important lessons and life principles did you learn from your parents? (If you were not raised by your parents, answer regarding what you learned from the family members or guardians who raised you.)

Read: Proverbs 12:15, Proverbs 12:26, and Proverbs 27:17

> *The way of a fool seems right to him,*
> *but a wise man listens to advice.* —Proverbs 12:15

> *The godly give good advice to their friends;*
> *the wicked lead them astray.* —Proverbs 12:26 (NLT)

> *As iron sharpens iron, so one man*
> *sharpens another.* —Proverbs 27:17

Question 3 : According to these verses, it's important to have godly, wise friends who can give us good advice and help "sharpen" us. Do you have friends who offer to speak the truth to you regarding your life and your decisions? How do you typically respond when the message is difficult to hear?

_____

_____

_____

 Read: 2 Timothy 3:16

All Scripture is God-breathed and is useful for teaching, rebuking,
correcting and training in righteousness... —2 Timothy 3:16

Question 4 : What important lessons have you learned from reading the Bible? Below, write down a few lessons you have learned, along with the associated Bible verses. How did these biblical teachings change your life and your behavior?

Question 5 : You can learn lessons from a number of different teachers, including trials (difficulties in life), mature Christian teachers, Bible verses, godly friends, parents, and other family members. This four-week study is about grace, so in this question you will focus on learning to show God's love and grace. In the chart below, for each category of "teacher," write down one or more specific ways in which you could (in the next month or two) learn to better extend grace to the people around you. The first row is an example.

TEACHER	HOW I CAN LEARN TO SHOW LOVE AND GRACE
ADVICE FROM FRIENDS	Meet with a few trusted Christian friends and ask them how well I show God's love and grace to others. Commit to improvement based on their advice. Other ways:
PARENTS AND OTHER FAMILY MEMBERS	
TRIALS IN MY LIFE *(think of some you're facing right now)*	
CHRISTIAN TEACHERS *(e.g., your pastor, small group leader, elders, etc.)*	
THE BIBLE	

PRAYER FOR GRACE

"Lord, I am so grateful that you are a loving, gracious God, and that you teach me and help me to change and grow to be more like your Son. I have not earned your love or your forgiveness, and yet you freely offer both to me. You are a perfect Father, and I thank you that you discipline me and bring situations and people into my life that are for my good. God, I pray that you reveal to me the lessons you want to teach me, and show me any way in which I might have resisted those lessons. I pray that you help me to see the teachers and lessons before me, and that you soften any resistance I might feel. Lord, show me how the trials in my life will help me to mature and become complete, not lacking anything. Give me wisdom to choose godly friends and teachers who will help me to grow my faith in obedience to your Word and your purpose in my life. Lord, bless me this week and teach me to follow you closely. This I pray in Christ's name. Amen."

Notes

WEEK 4:
GRACE IN **ACTION**

THIS WEEK'S QUOTE
FROM THE GRACE CARD:

"Dr. King used to tell us that Sunday morning in church is the locker room. Monday through Saturday out in the world? That's the game."

— Grandpa George talking to Sam

THIS WEEK'S SCRIPTURE:

Then Jesus came to them and said, "All authority in heaven and on earth has been given to me. Therefore go and make disciples of all nations, baptizing them in the name of the Father and of the Son and of the Holy Spirit, and teaching them to obey everything I have commanded you. And surely I am with you always, to the very end of the age."

— Matthew 28:18–20

GRACE IN **ACTION**

Open your study with prayer.

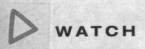

THE GRACE CARD
QUESTION FOR THE WEEK

If you could do anything you wanted in order to make the
world a better place, what would you do? Explain the
reasons for your choice.

▷ **WATCH**

Watch the Week 4 movie clip on the DVD in *The Grace Card*
DVD-based Study.

River Walk With Sam and Grandpa George *(2½ minutes)*
Sam is frustrated over being partnered with Mac, a man who
appears to dislike everyone who is different from him. Mac's
anger and bitter attitude toward life is the opposite of Sam's
joyful demeanor. On top of that, Sam is now starting to question
his calling as a pastor. The prior Sunday, Sam delivered a
message to his church in which he confessed his frustration
with Mac and his inability to love others as Jesus does. Sam also
told his congregation that they weren't any better than he was
at loving others. As you can imagine, that didn't go over well.
As Sam walks along the banks of the Mississippi River with his
grandfather George, he's about to learn an important life lesson
from his mentor—although it might take a while to sink in.

River walk with Sam and Grandpa George

STUDY AND **DISCUSS**

Read: Matthew 28:16–20

Then the eleven disciples went to Galilee, to the mountain where Jesus had told them to go. When they saw him, they worshiped him; but some doubted. Then Jesus came to them and said, "All authority in heaven and on earth has been given to me. Therefore go and make disciples of all nations, baptizing them in the name of the Father and of the Son and of the Holy Spirit, and teaching them to obey everything I have commanded you. And surely I am with you always, to the very end of the age." —Matthew 28:16–20

Question 1: In what ways do you see some Christians and/or the Church as a whole "staying in the locker room" rather than "getting into the game"? Does "the locker room" or "the playing field" best describe the focus of the church you attend?

_____

_____

_____

_____

This passage in Matthew takes us into the disciples' world in the aftermath of Jesus Christ's crucifixion and resurrection. The disciples have just gone through the shock and despair of seeing their Master and Teacher killed in the most painful, humiliating way possible in the ancient world. Three days later, they see prophecy fulfilled and hope returned through Jesus' resurrection from the tomb. Through His blood and sacrifice, Jesus has provided undeniable proof that He is indeed the Son of God—and our Lord and Savior.

Now the disciples are gathered together in the area of Galilee, the location of most of Jesus' ministry. In this Bible passage, Jesus is about to ascend to Heaven, back to His Father's side. Before He leaves, Jesus delivers final instructions to His followers, including this command to make disciples of all nations. Jesus' words in Matthew 28:19–20 are known as The Great Commission.

Question 2 : Would you describe yourself as someone who "gets into the game"? How comfortable and/or willing are you to talk with other people about your faith in Jesus?

_____

_____

_____

Question 3 : In what ways do you apply what you learn in the "locker room" at church to your life, Monday through Saturday? How do you use God's "game plan" to change the lives of the people around you? Give some recent examples.

_____

_____

_____

If you're still growing in this area, give some examples you've seen in the lives of other Christians. What can you learn from them?

_____

_____

_____

Grandpa George tells Sam that as a civil rights leader in Memphis, he learned from Dr. Martin Luther King about the importance of getting in the game instead of sitting in the locker room. The locker room is where the game plan is delivered—on Sundays in the sanctuary of the church. While it's critically important to gather together as a body of believers, and to grow and learn together, the actual game is played Monday through Saturday on the streets! After hearing the game plan in the locker room, we have to "get into the game!"

Read: 1 Peter 4:8–10 and Ephesians 2:10

Above all, love each other deeply, because love covers over a multitude of sins. Offer hospitality to one another without grumbling. Each one should use whatever gift he has received to serve others, faithfully administering God's grace in its various forms. —1 Peter 4:8–10

For we are God's workmanship, created in Christ Jesus to do good works, which God prepared in advance for us to do. —Ephesians 2:10

Question 4: In what ways are you demonstrating or sharing the grace of God with others? How could you increase your impact in this area?

_____

_____

_____

_____

Question 5: Think about the uniqueness of your personality and the gifts and talents God has given you. What do you love to do, and what are you good at? List those interests and abilities below.

_____

_____

_____

Question 6: How specifically are you using the gifts you just listed to "do good works" in God's kingdom? Are there other ways in which you could reach people for Jesus using your gifts and talents?

_____

_____

_____

 Read: Matthew 4:18–20 and Acts 2:22–41

> As Jesus was walking beside the Sea of Galilee, he saw two brothers, Simon called Peter and his brother Andrew. They were casting a net into the lake, for they were fishermen. "Come, follow me," Jesus said, "and I will make you fishers of men." At once they left their nets and followed him.   —Matthew 4:18–20

> Those who accepted his message were baptized, and about three thousand were added to their number that day.   —Acts 2:41

Sea of Galilee

STEP INTO THE
PASSAGE

Simon (later called Peter) was a young, uneducated fisherman from the Jewish town of Bethsaida. He was outspoken, impatient, and full of bluster. Simon was the disciple who tried to walk on water, then lost his courage and sank at Jesus' feet. He was the follower of Jesus who fell asleep in the Garden of Gethsemane when his Master asked him to watch and pray. He was also the disciple who denied knowing Jesus after His arrest.

But Jesus saw beyond those flaws. In John 1:42, when Jesus first met Simon, Jesus looked at him and said, "You are Simon son of John. You will be called Cephas…" In ancient Jewish culture, names were frequently descriptive of a person, and both *Cephas* (Aramaic) and *Peter* (Greek) mean "rock." Jesus saw not only who Simon was, but also who he would *become*—the courageous, natural leader whose passion and overflowing of the Holy Spirit drew thousands of new believers to the early Church. Jesus re-named him "Peter," and he lived for approximately thirty years after Jesus' resurrection. Peter died by crucifixion under the Roman emperor Nero.

Question 7: Read the Step Into the Passage section on the Apostle Peter and think about the two Scriptures you've just read. What do you think of the dramatic way Jesus' promise to Peter (to make him a "fisher of men") was fulfilled?

_____

_____

_____

Question 8: In one day, Peter inspired three thousand people to enter into an eternal relationship with Christ. What would it be like to arrive in Heaven and see people you had led to Jesus? How would you feel?

_____

_____

_____

THE GRACE CARD
LESSON

 Re-read: Matthew 28:16-20

Then the eleven disciples went to Galilee, to the mountain where Jesus had told them to go. When they saw him, they worshiped him; but some doubted. Then Jesus came to them and said, "All authority in heaven and on earth has been given to me. Therefore go and make disciples of all nations, baptizing them in the name of the Father and of the Son and of the Holy Spirit, and teaching them to obey everything I have commanded you. And surely I am with you always, to the very end of the age." —Matthew 28:16-20

Read the following lesson to yourself, or if you're doing the study as a group, ask one or more of the group members to read the lesson out loud.

Of all the things Jesus could have said to His disciples before He left them forever, these are the final words He gives them. Jesus tells His followers to "go and make disciples…" In essence, He is saying, "Get into the game! Don't wait for the tired and weary to come to you—*go to them* and make disciples!" For many of us in today's churches, we would rather worship with fellow believers than go into the streets to reach non-believers. But without us going into the world—and getting into the game—who will point people to Jesus?

The goal of a Jesus-follower is to make disciples. The more people you reach, encourage, and help develop a mature faith, the more the Kingdom of God (and the Church) will grow—in both numbers and strength.

In the same way that athletes need to train so they can perform at their best, we need a steady diet of worship, Bible study, prayer, and fellowship at a church in order to reach and impact non-believers. One of the mistakes believers often make is not getting their own "batteries" charged with a fresh anointing from God. This is accomplished in and through worship with the body of Christ. And if you're a new believer yourself, look for those in the church who can encourage and mentor you. Is there someone who can be a "Grandpa George" to you and teach you a few life lessons?

Even though we need a regular time of renewal at church, we can't get into the game if we stay in the locker room. Mark your calendar like this—Sunday (and other times of small group study and worship): Locker room talk, encouragement, strategy. Monday through Saturday: Game time!

When those who are floundering in life see joy and passion in a committed follower of Christ, a hunger is ignited within them. But how many people will walk into our churches—our locker rooms—to catch a glimpse of that joy? Our passion and joy are best seen by others when we get into the game during the week, when we live our lives intentionally with the goal of reaching our communities with the love of God and an invitation to follow Christ!

In Matthew 4:19, Jesus began His ministry by calling His disciples to become "fishers of men." The term "apostle" means "sent one" or "one who is sent away." Are we doing enough to impact others, or is our focus on the locker room? God is calling us to get into the game!

STUDY
AND **DISCUSS**

 Read: John 3:16 and Luke 16:19-31

"For God so loved the world that he gave his one and only Son, that whoever believes in him shall not perish but have eternal life." —John 3:16

"He answered, 'Then I beg you, father, send Lazarus to my father's house, for I have five brothers. Let him warn them, so that they will not also come to this place of torment.'" —Luke 16:27-28

Question 9: How does the rich man react when he realizes the end result of the choices he made in his life? Whom does he want to warn and why?

_____

_____

_____

Question 10: Jesus came to the world so that we could spend eternity with God in Heaven. As you read this parable about the rich man, what does it say about the cost of not sharing your faith with the people in your life? Talk in your group about the importance of sharing Jesus with others. How does this Bible passage increase your sense of urgency?

_____

_____

_____

If you have not already accepted Jesus as your Lord and Savior, you can do that today. Or, if you've been a Christian but you've drifted away from God, take this opportunity to re-commit your life to Him. Talk to your group leader if you would like to pray to receive Jesus or if you've made a commitment to re-dedicate your life to Christ. Sharing your decision with other Christians is one of the best ways to stick with your commitment and grow in your relationship with God.

*Ask group members to share prayer requests,
and then close your study with prayer.*

REMEMBER TO COMPLETE THE **ON MY OWN** SECTION
LATER THIS WEEK.

ON MY OWN

We're not the first people God called to get into the game.
As we've seen in this week's lesson, He's done it with His
people throughout the course of history. The people He called
weren't necessarily the most popular, the strongest, the best
equipped, or even the most willing! But you can read story
after story in the Bible about people who stepped out in faith
and got into the game in a way that changed the world around
them. What can we learn from their examples? Consider these
four Get Into the Game profiles of people in the Bible.

GRACE IN ACTION PROFILES

*Note: We encourage you to read all four profiles, but if you are short on time, you may
choose one profile. After you've read the profile(s), go to the Grace in Action Studies (starting
on page 68) and complete the readings and study questions in that section.*

THE APOSTLE PETER

WHO WAS HE?	We met the Apostle Peter earlier in this lesson. While all Jewish boys were taught to know the Torah (the Old Testament portion of the Bible), there's nothing in the four Gospels that indicates that Peter was particularly knowledgeable about the Word of God—or about how to run a new, rapidly growing church! After Jesus' ascension, the apostles John and Peter appeared before the Sanhedrin (the ruling Jewish authority), and the reaction of those leaders is recorded in Acts 4:13: *"When they saw the courage of Peter and John and realized that they were unschooled, ordinary men, they were astonished and they took note that these men had been with Jesus."*

HE WAS CALLED TO…	… do something big for which he wasn't qualified. When Jesus called Peter to get into the game, do you think the people who knew Peter believed he was qualified? Do you think they thought he was the best person to build a new church in the midst of his unbelief, the resistance of the Jewish religious leaders, and even deadly persecution? Yet, Jesus chose him!
THE CALL	*"And I tell you that you are Peter, and on this rock I will build my church, and the gates of Hades will not overcome it."* — Matthew 16:18
HIS RESPONSE	He left the life of a fisherman and became one of Jesus' twelve apostles. After Jesus' resurrection, Peter fearlessly spoke the good news of the Gospel, built the Christian Church in Israel, and eventually gave his life for his faith.
HOW HE CHANGED THE GAME	Peter led thousands of people to Christ and was the leader of the early Christian church. The Holy Spirit Himself transformed, empowered, and equipped Peter to be the church leader Christ desired him to be. That same transforming power is available to all who will completely surrender their life to Jesus Christ and be a vessel for that power to flow *through*.

THE APOSTLE PAUL

WHO WAS HE?	A Roman citizen from the city of Tarsus, Paul (first named Saul) was a strict Pharisee (religious leader) who had studied under the Rabbi Gamaliel, the leading religious authority of the time. Saul was zealous about destroying the Christian Church, which he viewed as preaching heresy against the Jewish religion. He persecuted, arrested, and killed Christians. After a dramatic conversion on the road to Damascus in which he saw Jesus, Saul was renamed Paul and joined the growing Christian Church.
HE WAS CALLED TO…	… change from an enemy of the Church into one of its leaders— and be greatly forgiven in the process.
THE CALL	*As he neared Damascus on his journey, suddenly a light from heaven flashed around him. He fell to the ground and heard a voice say to him, "Saul, Saul, why do you persecute me?"* *"Who are you, Lord?" Saul asked.* *"I am Jesus, whom you are persecuting," he replied. "Now get up and go into the city, and you will be told what you must do."* — Acts 9:3-6

HIS RESPONSE	Paul set aside everything he had previously believed about God and the identity of Jesus and dedicated his life to sharing the Gospel.
HOW HE CHANGED THE GAME	Paul was the leading evangelist to the Gentiles (non-Jews) and was instrumental in training Christian leaders and starting new churches throughout Israel, Turkey, Greece, and Italy. He was such an enthusiastic activist for the cause of Christ that he was eventually arrested and placed in a Roman prison. From there, Paul wrote thirteen of the twenty-seven books that now comprise the New Testament. These God-inspired, authoritative letters not only address issues relevant to us today, but they also teach us how to live a life completely committed to Christ.

GIDEON

WHO WAS HE?	Gideon lived in the time of the judges, one to two centuries before King David ruled Israel. In the seven years prior to the story of Gideon (recorded in Judges 6–8), the Midianites and other peoples living to the East had been invading Israel. The invaders destroyed the Israelites' crops and livestock, leaving God's people poor and desperate. The Israelites cried out to God, and God sent an angel to call Gideon, the "least" member of his family, which was from the weakest clan.
HE WAS CALLED TO…	… do something impossible! The angel commanded Gideon to lead the Israelites against the Midianites. But first, God had Gideon reduce the size of his army to only three hundred men. The Israelites were to fight against an enemy the Bible says was as "thick as locusts." Only God could bring victory out of such an impossible situation!
THE CALL	*When the angel of the LORD appeared to Gideon, he said, "The LORD is with you, mighty warrior."* — Judges 6:12 *The LORD turned to him and said, "Go in the strength you have and save Israel out of Midian's hand. Am I not sending you?"* — Judges 6:14
HIS RESPONSE	Gideon asked the angel for reassurance and questioned him about why God had allowed the Midianites to oppress the people of Israel. Then Gideon asked for three signs to prove God was with him. In the end, Gideon obeyed and led the Israelites into battle against their Eastern enemies.
HOW HE CHANGED THE GAME	God enabled Gideon and the Israelites to defeat their enemies, and the Israelites had forty years of peace.

ESTHER

WHO WAS SHE?	Esther lived in Susa, in the Persian Empire, during a time when the Israelites had been exiled from their own country. After King Xerxes rejected his queen, the king's servants had beautiful young virgins from all over the land brought to the king's harem. The Bible says that Esther "won the favor of all who saw her." Of all the young women in his harem, King Xerxes chose Esther as his new queen.
SHE WAS CALLED TO…	… do something that took great courage! When an enemy of the Jews convinced King Xerxes to destroy the Jewish people, Esther's cousin Mordecai called her to go into the king's presence to ask for mercy for the Jews. But in Persia, the law forbade anyone to approach the king without being summoned, and the penalty for disobeying the law was death.
THE CALL	*He also gave him a copy of the text of the edict for their annihilation, which had been published in Susa, to show to Esther and explain it to her, and he told him to urge her to go into the king's presence to beg for mercy and plead with him for her people.* — Esther 4:8 *"For if you remain silent at this time, relief and deliverance for the Jews will arise from another place, but you and your father's family will perish. And who knows but that you have come to your royal position for such a time as this?"* — Esther 4:14
HER RESPONSE	*Then Esther sent this reply to Mordecai: "Go, gather together all the Jews who are in Susa, and fast for me. Do not eat or drink for three days, night or day. I and my maids will fast as you do. When this is done, I will go to the king, even though it is against the law. And if I perish, I perish."* — Esther 4:15–16 Esther fasted, prayed, and then approached King Xerxes through a God-inspired plan.
HOW SHE CHANGED THE GAME	Esther's courageous response to God's call saved the lives of thousands of Jews. The Jewish people still celebrate a holiday called Purim to commemorate their deliverance in the time of Esther.

Choose one of the four profiles. Choose the person who most inspires you or with whom you most closely identify. For example, if you feel like you've done sinful things that would prevent you from being used by God, choose the Apostle Paul. Or, if you are inspired by the courage of Esther, choose her.

Now, go to the Grace in Action Studies (next page) and find the name of the profile you've chosen (i.e., go to the section labeled "Esther" if you've chosen Esther). Complete the readings and study questions in that section.

Apostle Peter

 Read about Peter in these Bible passages:

Matthew 14:25–31, Matthew 16:13–19, Matthew 26:69–75,
John 21:4–7, Acts 4:8–13, and Acts 5:12–16

Question 1: What do you like about the Apostle Peter?
What were some of his faults? In what ways do you identify
with him?

The excavated remains of Peter's house in Capernaum
Photo courtesy of Todd Bolen, BiblePlaces.com

Question 2: Do you feel
qualified to serve God and
make disciples? Why or
why not?

Question 3: Describe how Peter went from being
unqualified for his task to making an incredible difference
in the world. What (or who) made him qualified to build
Jesus' church?

Read: Zechariah 4:6 and Job 42:1-2

So he said to me, "This is the word of the LORD to Zerubbabel: 'Not by might nor by power, but by my Spirit,' says the LORD Almighty. —Zechariah 4:6

Then Job replied to the LORD: "I know that you can do all things; no plan of yours can be thwarted." —Job 42:1-2

Question 4: According to these verses, does God provide the strength and power to accomplish His purposes, or do you? How does that make a difference?

Question 5: Knowing that God will provide the wisdom, strength, and power required to accomplish His plans, what can you do to put grace in action and make an impact in God's kingdom? List some specific steps you're going to take in the next few weeks.

 PRAYER FOR **GRACE**

"Lord, you are a keeper of promises, and I know you have promised to give me wisdom, to strengthen me, and to accomplish your plans through your power and through your Spirit working in my life. Give me courage to get into the game, to take specific steps to reach people for you, and to make disciples for your kingdom. While I may not be qualified, I know you use the weak and the humble to accomplish great things. Empower me through your Holy Spirit, guide me, and give me opportunities to share the good news of your Gospel. I trust you; I am yours, and I pray for you to bless others through me and to accomplish amazing things through my life. Thank you for your love and for your grace. Amen."

Apostle Paul

 Read about Paul in these Bible passages:

Acts 7:54–8:3, Acts 9:3–6 & 26–29, 1 Corinthians 15:3–10, 2 Timothy 4:6–8

Question 1: What do you like about the Apostle Paul? What were some of his faults? In what ways do you identify with him?

_____

_____

_____

Question 2: How greatly did Paul/Saul sin against God and hurt the Christian Church? Is there anything in the passages you just read that tells you Paul was aware of his sin? What did he say about it?

_____

_____

_____

Question 3: Have you ever felt like you have made too many mistakes to be used by God? If so, why?

_____

_____

_____

 Read: Romans 5:6–8, 2 Corinthians 5:17–21, and 1 John 1:9

But God demonstrates his own love for us in this: While we were still sinners, Christ died for us.   —Romans 5:8

Therefore, if anyone is in Christ, he is a new creation; the old has gone, the new has come! All this is from God, who reconciled us to himself through Christ and gave us the ministry of reconciliation: that God was reconciling the world to himself in Christ, not counting men's sins against them.   —2 Corinthians 5:17–19a

*If we confess our sins, he is faithful and just and will forgive us our sins
and purify us from all unrighteousness.   —1 John 1:9*

Question 4: What concepts or promises from these
passages stand out to you? What does it mean to you to be
a "new creation"?

_____

_____

_____

Question 5: Knowing that as a Christian you are forgiven
and a new creation, what can you do to put grace in action
and make an impact in God's kingdom? List some specific
steps you're going to take in the next few weeks.

_____

_____

_____

PRAYER FOR GRACE

*"Lord, I thank you for your love, your grace, and your
forgiveness. I am so grateful that you have changed me
and that I can be a new creation, with hope for a better
life and an eternity with you. Please continue to guide me
and to make me more like you. Lord, help me learn from
your grace and forgiveness. Help me to forgive myself,
and enable me to see others through your eyes. Pour your
love and your Spirit into me, and help me to love others
and offer them grace. Lord, I am your creation and your
servant. I pray for you to bless others through me and to
accomplish amazing things through my life. Amen."*

Gideon

 Read about Gideon in this Bible passage:

Judges 6–8

Question 1: What do you like about Gideon? What were some of his faults? In what ways do you identify with him?

_____

_____

_____

Question 2: Why do you think Gideon doubted the angel and questioned him? How did God respond to Gideon's doubts and need for reassurance?

_____

_____

_____

Question 3: Have you ever had doubts about God—either about His existence, His plans, or His willingness to accomplish good through your life? How did you handle your doubts?

_____

_____

_____

_____

Re-Read: *Judges 6–8*

Question 4: According to the angel, how much strength did Gideon need in order to respond to God's call? What assurance did Gideon receive in Judges 6:16? How do these verses relate to your own life and to your ability to get into the game?

_____

_____

_____

Read: Mark 9:17–27, Matthew 28:20b

Immediately the boy's father exclaimed, "I do believe;
help me overcome my unbelief!" —Mark 9:24

"And surely I am with you always, to the
very end of the age." —Matthew 28:20b

Question 5: Knowing that God is with you and will empower you to accomplish His plans, what can you do to put grace in action? List some specific steps you're going to take in the next few weeks.

_____

_____

_____

 ## PRAYER FOR GRACE

"Lord, forgive me for the times that I doubt and for the times that I hesitate to share my faith and reach out to others. Thank you for your patience and for helping me with my unbelief. I am so grateful for your promise that you are always with me, even to the end of the age. Thank you for your strength and your presence, and thank you for allowing me to be a part of your plans. Lord, I pray for you to give me opportunities to go into the world in your name. Lord, pour your love and your spirit into me, and help me to love others and offer them grace. I pray for you to bless others through me and to accomplish amazing things through my life. Amen."

Esther

 Read about Esther in this Bible passage:

Esther 3–7 (If you have time, read the whole book of Esther.)

Question 1 : What do you like about Esther? What do you think about how she handled the situation in which she found herself? In what ways do you identify with her?

_____

_____

_____

Question 2 : In what ways did Mordecai influence Esther? In there anyone in your life who encourages you to have faith and to get into the game? Who is that person and how do they impact your life?

_____

_____

_____

Question 3 : If you were to share your faith and to stand for what you believe, is there any risk that you might face rejection, loss of position or property, or even some type of harm? Explain.

_____

_____

_____

 Read: Esther 4:15–16, Joshua 1:9, and Philippians 4:6–7

Then Esther sent this reply to Mordecai: "Go, gather together all the Jews who are in Susa, and fast for me. Do not eat or drink for three days, night or day. I and my maids will fast as you do. When this is done, I will go to the king, even though it is against the law. And if I perish, I perish."   —Esther 4:15–16

"Have I not commanded you? Be strong and courageous. Do not be terrified; do not be discouraged, for the LORD your God will be with you wherever you go." —Joshua 1:9

Do not be anxious about anything, but in everything, by prayer and petition, with thanksgiving, present your requests to God. And the peace of God, which transcends all understanding, will guard your hearts and your minds in Christ Jesus. —Philippians 4:6–7

Question 4: According to Esther 4:15–16, what did Esther do before she approached the king? When you pray, what types of things do you ask God for? How often do you ask Him for the wisdom and courage to do His will?

_____

_____

_____

Question 5: After reading Esther's inspiring story, what can you do to put grace in action? List some specific steps you're going to take in the next few weeks.

_____

_____

_____

 ## PRAYER FOR GRACE

"Lord, thank you for your promise that you are always with me. Forgive me for the times when I am fearful and when I allow my anxious thoughts to hold me back from doing your work. Thank you that you have the power to protect me, that you go before me, and that the battle is yours. Lord, when I look for help, I know that my help comes from the Maker of heaven and earth. You are holy and powerful, and nothing can stand against you or your plans. Thank you for your strength and your presence. Lord, pour your love and your Spirit into me, and help me to love others and offer them grace. I pray for you to bless others through me and to accomplish amazing things through my life. Amen."

Notes

THE GRACE CARD
DVD-BASED STUDY

Experience a grace awakening with this four-week study!

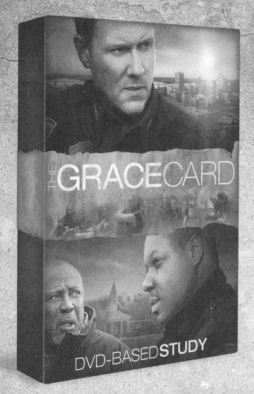

THE GRACE CARD DVD-BASED STUDY

is founded on life-changing, biblical principles of forgiveness and love. Engage in a four-week study using exclusive movie clips from *The Grace Card*, relevant Bible verses, questions for group discussion, and four thought-provoking Bible lessons.

This all-inclusive kit provides everything you need for individual or group study:

- DVD with *The Grace Card* movie clips for each lesson
- Study Guide that features an easy-to-use format, high-quality graphics, and Bible-based lessons
- Leader's Guide with tips for each lesson and instructions for leading a great small group

Look for *The Grace Card* **DVD-Based Study** at your local Christian bookstore, or visit Outreach.com for bulk quantities.